Last Wishes

LAST WISHES

POEMS BY

Rob Wright

ABLE MUSE PRESS

Able Muse Press

www.ablemusepress.com

Library of Congress Cataloging-in-Publication Data

Names: Wright, Rob, 1953- author.
Title: Last Wishes / Poems by Rob Wright.
Description: San Jose, CA : Able Muse Press, 2020.
Identifiers: LCCN 2020000569 (print) | LCCN 2020000570 (ebook) | ISBN
    9781773490700 (paperback) | ISBN 9781773490717 (digital)
Subjects: LCGFT: Poetry.
Classification: LCC PS3623.R5637 L37 2020 (print) | LCC PS3623.R5637 (ebook)
    | DDC 811/.6--dc23
LC record available at https://lccn.loc.gov/2020000569
LC ebook record available at https://lccn.loc.gov/2020000570

Printed in the United States of America

Cover image: *Edge of Shadows* by Alexander Pepple
            (with *Entrance* by Skeeze and *Vent* by Jennifer Ditscheit)

Cover & book design by Alexander Pepple

Rob Wright photo (page 69) by Tom Goodman

Able Muse Press is an imprint of *Able Muse:* A Review of Poetry, Prose & Art—at
www.ablemuse.com

Able Muse Press
467 Saratoga Avenue #602
San Jose, CA 95129

For Suzan

With all your lost grief,
what I can give.
Dear lord of the fields. . . .

—James Dickey

Acknowledgments

My grateful acknowledgments go to the editors of the following publications where these poems, some in earlier versions, first appeared:

Able Muse: "She asked if I could talk about my past," "Somerset, 1972," and "Strange Obsequies"

Angle: "Before the Papal Visit, 2015" and "Forest for the Trees"

Big City Lit: "Bankrupt Farms," "Elegy for Maureen Holm," "In a Room of Quaker Plainness," "Photograph, W. H. Auden, 1972," "To the Horse on Queen Lane," and "Song"

The Evansville Review: "Meetings with My Father" (i–iv)

The Guardian: "A Skinful"

Measure: "Last Wish"

Schuylkill Valley Journal: "Photograph, Liberia, 1980"

String Poet: "At the Eastern Pennsylvania Psychiatric Institute," "Majdanek 1995," and "Manhattan, 1987"

For the past nine years, I've been privileged to have Rob Wright among those sitting around the table in one of the writing workshops that I lead. All this time we have cheered him on (as he has cheered us on, in equal measure), and we are delighted at the publication of *Last Wishes* and the opportunity it presents to share him with a larger audience. Though this is Wright's first collection of poems, he is hardly new to the craft. From the time a high school teacher encouraged him to write poetry, and he discovered Robert's Frost's "Out, Out," and "Acquainted with the Night," he has spent a lifetime steeped in poetry.

From Wright's biography, it is not hard to see how "Acquainted with Night" might speak to him. Wright was born on a farm in Western Pennsylvania. After Wright's mother left an abusive marriage to a wealthy and powerful man, she and Wright and his sister were left to fall back on their own resources. Wright went to work in a factory in Western Pennsylvania to earn money for college (an experience related in "Somerset, 1972"). He studied photography at the Philadelphia College for Art, switched his major to film, and worked for three decades in film production, on projects including Jonathan Demme's *Philadelphia* and *Pola's March*, the documentary of a Holocaust survivor (the poem "Majdanek, 1995" comes out of this experience). During his years in film he wrote little, but after a bout with pneumonia laid him in bed for two weeks, he started writing again and hasn't looked back since: poetry, fiction, reviews, and novels. Appropriately, in 2014, he won the Frost Farm Prize for Metrical Poetry, and gave a reading at the Frost Farm in Derry, New Hampshire.

My primary job here, however, is not to tell you the life or list the awards, but to cut a path to the poetry. Wright's work is worldly, in the best sense of the word. His career has taken him all over the globe. But more than that, he has the soul and sensibility of a traveler. We see here a youth who says, of a beacon, "How I'd like to grip / that light and ride its circuit," and who, in "Falls Cut, 1970," jumps a freight train. Think of the keen eye of Basho, where details of the external world mix with internal images to form a greater whole.

We find here searing spiritual questions, about God and what religion or belief can ultimately offer, about despair ("Mount Holly, 2015," "At the Basilica of Saints Peter and Paul," "Past Imperfect," "Between the Hours," "Strange Obsequies"). We also find what Louise Glück has called "conversation with the great dead" (the series of "Photograph" poems, of W.H. Auden, Anne Sexton, Francis Bacon, in addition to more than one friend lost along the way).

One of Wright's gifts is the age-old poetic magic of conveying beauty in what might at first appear to offer up nothing but ugliness. Witness the sestina "Bankrupt Farms," in which the horrorscape of an abandoned farm and a dead and pregnant feral dog is conveyed in accurate and yet somehow sumptuous language. His cinematically trained eye shows in his ability to render complexities in visual tableaux. It is fitting that one of the titles here is "Prologue for an Imaginary Play," because Wright's poems often are, in essence, little plays. The landscapes here are never static; like a photographer, or a cinematographer, Wright captures his subjects at their most revealing in a flash. Scenes are arranged and rendered at the moment of greatest drama and tension.

The quality of tenacity also comes to mind, with humility and compassion closely trailing. Wright's history and poems have in common a story of survival. Wright has seen plenty, and comes back to tell honestly what he has seen and felt. In "Twelve Steps," he describes the sound of a voice attempting to articulate its journey:

> It travels from the root up to the tongue
> and past the teeth. In here it's known as truth
> and slippery, unlike plain honesty,
> the naked lady with the crooked back.

Wright often, though not exclusively, writes in conventional forms. As in the best formal poetry, the form never calls undue attention to itself: the form works to enhance the language, and language is never deformed for the purposes of merely filling out the form. In fact, one of the greatest pleasures of Wright's work is to read a poem and only after reading realizing that it's written in form.

One of my favorite poems in *Last Wishes* is "To the Horse on Queen Lane," in which we return to those beginnings on a Western Pennsylvania farm. "A man whose face / is lost to memory" breaks a cigarette into the young boy's hands and lifts him above the fence to feed it to a horse:

> A mouth dips down and picks
> tobacco, strand by strand, with yellow teeth.
>
> Each nostril's like a tunnel in a dream,
> and underneath the massive chin are hairs
> that bristle at my touch. A man whose face
> is lost to memory now lifts me up
> above the fence to touch. . . .
> . . . .
>   my first
> clear memory, on Queen Lane, standing on
> the frost-heaved earth, with you, my nameless mare.

So many moments of the poems in this collection stay with me: ferns and creeks of Western Pennsylvania, waxing boots for wear on the factory floor, the blood in the sink of a hunter's father's kitchen, feral children behind a fence in Sao Paolo, the furniture in a psychiatrist's office. I could go on listing, but I am hoping that this taste will encourage you to read and experience these images for yourself.

Alison Hicks
Los Angeles, California
March 2020

Contents

ix   Foreword

3   She asked if I could talk about my past, so I replied,

4   Lambertsville, 1965

7   Falls Cut, 1970

8   Fort Meyers, 1971

9   Somerset, 1972

10   Manhattan, 1986

11   Kowloon, 1993

12   São Paulo, 1994

13   Majdanek, 1995

15   Mount Holly, 2015

16   At the Basilica of Saints Peter and Paul

18   Before the Papal Visit, 2015

19   At the Eastern Pennsylvania Psychiatric Institute

22   Motel, Date Unknown

23   Twelve Steps

24   Forest for the Trees

25   To the Horse on Queen Lane

26   For John

27   "The hours are hung with clouds, not flags"

28   For Christine

30   Past Imperfect

32 A Skinful

34 Photograph, W. H. Auden, 1972

35 Photograph, Anne Sexton, 1973

36 Photograph, T. S. Eliot, 1932

37 In a Room of Quaker Plainness

39 Photograph, Liberia, 1980

42 Fall Back

44 Bankrupt Farms

46 Prologue for an Imaginary Play

48 August 1963

50 September 11, 1973

52 Song

54 Old Bones

55 An Early Recording

56 Between the Hours

58 Strange Obsequies

60 Elegy for Maureen Holm

61 Meetings with My Father

67 Last Wish

Last Wishes

She asked if I could talk about my past, so I replied,

Where I grew up the mines were working still.
And trucks roared down the narrow roads and heaved
cinders into ditches, ferns, and weeds.
The mines were then big craters where the earth
was scraped away and heaped on barren hills,
all night and every night. And I could feel
the dull vibration pulsing through the floor
as giant shovels chewed through clay and slate.

Before my time, the mines were shafts and holes.
A friend found rusted miner's lamps inside
a shed his uncle kept for garden tools.
And as I turned them in my hands I thought
how hunger drives a man to crawl beneath
the brittle crust that shuts out sun and sky.

Lambertsville, 1965

i

The shadows of the trees inch up the lawn.
I toe my sneakers to the ragged edge
and watch the line flow up and then retreat,
like waves breaking along a hot green shore.
This is the boundary I always cross:
from manicured to lush, from tame to wild,
through elderberries, brambles, sassafras,
like wading through rough breakers to the sea.

Now I'm beneath the canopy of leaves,
inside the cooling air. The mast of seed
sends signals to my nose—a lover's scent?
With every step I take into the dark
shelter of the sycamores and ash,
a languid, bitter smell draws me in deep.

ii

The older ones are thick and I am thin.
They often comment on this fact and say
that I have wings: twin scapulae that push
up though the freckled skin across my spine.
I watch the thick ones mix their drinks with ice,
and drag the scent of cigarettes and age
in slipstreams as they pass by me to sit
on furniture indented by their weight.

Come with me and I'll lead you through this house,
past beds with sheets still damp with clinging musk,
and dark apartments built for maiden aunts.
Now put your head against this wall and hear
the sound of tiny animals that bore
through wooden beams, like time lapse in a film.

iii

On summer nights I see the beacon sweep
across the tops of trees. The beam is white
and glowing, like a cone of moving cream
that's beaten in a bowl until it peaks.
I count the seconds for the light to pass
and calculate the time it takes the beam
to travel round the tower as I watch
the flashing lights of aircraft circling.

Eight miles? The beacon sweeps around again—
so pure and silent. How I'd like to grip
that light and ride its circuit, looking down
on streetlights marking ribbons on the roads
and trailer parks, while television screens
pulse signals onto croaking frogs on lawns.

iv

I gauge my stride to match the rise and fall
of furrows scoured in the loam. The crack
of dried-up stubble underneath my boots
reminds me of those mornings when, alone,
I'd flush a pheasant out of fresh-mown hay.

The earth is torn. The clods I trample on
might have been churned by high explosive shells,
like, on the Somme half a century ago.

I think of poets sent to fight in France—
Blunden, Sassoon, Thomas, Robert Graves—
who lived or died in no-man's-land by chance.
Drizzle patters on my hood and face,
reminding me of verses written down
in weather made of white-hot, ripping steel.

Falls Cut, 1970

The rails tops have been polished to a sheen
so bright the kicked-back light can bruise my eyes.
I hop from rail to rail and feel the shock
as polished steel compresses bone to bone.
I listen for the clap of couplings
as railcar shunts to railcar–as they cross
the spur lines rolling through the points that ring
in echoes down the rows of empty cars.

I run beside a freight and gather speed,
then catch a ladder welded to a gap
between the clacking iron dragon's scales.
I taste the tang of metal, watch the ties
that strobe beneath my feet as shadows fall
from banks of cinders raised in paradise.

Fort Meyers, 1971

A bungalow just off the beach is now
inhabited by spirits, and I'm one.
It's odd to watch the family who've moved in
ignore the silent ghosts who stand and watch
patiently as children hose off sand
that clings to bellies. We can hear the sound
of adults as they turn in bed, caress
as sweating bodies cry in ecstasy.

We once lived here—the dealers hustling
a hit, the hidden Gospels, or the Tao.
Surfers who mowed lawns at trailer parks
still wax their boards out on the porch, although
they can't be seen, except in certain lights,
when storms blow off the Gulf of Mexico.

Somerset, 1972

I treated my old boots with paraffin,
and as I turned the seams above a flame
I watched the leather soak in melting wax
like dried-up earth absorbing summer rain.
But rather than preventing muck and sleet
from seeping through, the treated leather picked
up marl dug out from pits along the banks
of rivers dammed by ice and melting snow.

I found work in a factory that spring,
and there the wax absorbed hot burls of chrome
spit out from lathes and taps on late-night shifts.
Then, walking home alone, I liked to watch
the leather glitter as I passed the girls
who posed in vapor light on chain-linked streets.

Manhattan, 1986

A window washers' scaffold rests against
the cornices and windows slick with soap.
Above it, flags flap straight out in the wind,
untainted by the carpet of exhaust
that pools around the cars and trucks below.
I watch the workmen hanging high above
the dueling cabbies fighting for the lanes
and human masses pressing to the curbs.

Banks and law firms form a solid wall
built on the bones of movie palaces,
where once I sat beneath projected beams
that flickered in the smoke from cigarettes,
and watched the bobbing heads on broken seats—
the lovers drunk on images, the lost.

Kowloon, 1993

The airplane's cabin door swings up and breaks
the airlock, letting in the thickened air,
the kind you need to shove against to move.

Because this weight of air has passed across
a mass of forest, earth, and rock so vast,
it swallows massed invading armies whole,
it carries with it souls as well as dust.

And here it is, to welcome me again—
the sprawl of birth and age, the cricket lust,
and fungus drawn so deep into my lungs
it tricks my mind into remembrance of

those other late arrivals in a dusk
of vapor light and dancing gnats that fall
and scatter on the earth like living rain.

São Paulo, 1994

This city on the plane is named for Paul—
a saint who never washed up here. Its parks
are full of feral children passing time
by turning tricks and huffing up the fumes
of solvents passed in sacks from hand to hand.
Their faces are the color of the leaves
of philodendrons throwing shadows down
on supplicants going through the ritual
of making all existence sparkling.

I saw one every day on my commute
along the line of hustlers by the fence.
He never moved. It looked as if he'd grown
a mass of roots that held him to the clay
as red as beetroot sold in open stalls.

Majdanek, 1995

i

I pass a barracks filled with children's shoes.
That smell, so human, is still strong despite
the decades that have passed. What's frightening here
is everything was done so rationally:
the miles of tracks were laid; the fences rigged;
the temperature to render bone to dust
was calculated on a drawing board
by sober engineers.
                                    I'm not alone;
a mass of ghosts is starting at my boots
and pushing bony fingers though the wire.
As well as hunger in their eyes, there's rage.
They shiver on the frozen ground, as I
take photographs of crematoria
that turned their living bodies into ash.

ii

How odd to be a tourist here, to see
the searchlights, wooden towers, and coils of wire
in three dimensions, tinted brown with rust
instead of flat and grainy black and white.
All history's been reduced to clips of film
in montages I carry in my head.
I stop to take a picture of the stack
that once spit out gray ash onto the streets
and houses lined up on the ring of hills
that overlooked the camp.
                                    There's not a soul

that's visible, to kick a soccer ball
or tend the flapping laundry stretched on lines.
The shadow of the smokestack sweeps the woods
to touch suburban lawns each afternoon.

iii

My watch is broken. No, it's time itself
that's slowed. I see the second hand move on
from point to point as if it's passing through
a medium much thicker than plain air.
To pass inside the boundaries of this world
of rusted fences, muck, and unmarked graves—
of fates dealt out in numbers staggering—
is risky; one can never quite return.

The images that I've recorded here,
mechanically, are pale compared to those
that come to me when I lie down and meet
the citizens of that metropolis
inside the borders of my dreaming head—
another place the dead can call their own.

Mount Holly, 2015

The priest shakes every hand as we file past.
His face is black in contrast to his robes.
His hand is hard and seems to swallow mine.
Peace be with you. I look into his eyes.
With you as well, I say to him. The phrase
is almost automatic, but not here,
with him—I want to break the ritual
and say, *Dear Father, do you realize*
that many in attendance here don't buy
your message, and believe that life's a sad,
strange drama that's played out in doubt and fear?
His grip has tightened, and his eyes are locked
uncomfortably on mine. There's movement there,
as if his soul were stirring in the sphere.

At the Basilica of Saints Peter and Paul

i

I'm told I must abject myself and kneel
in all humility and kiss the floor.
I can't do this, but take your Son's advice
and state my strange petitions in the dark.
Are you the trickster God, the one who showed
my ancestors the secret of how marks
drawn on a wall or written on a page
expose the shadows flickering inside?

Something suggests to me you're more than that—
for instance, there's your sense of irony:
The last shall be the first, etc. Now,
five billion sad requests fly up to you:
raw signals mixing high above the sphere:
the static that your children chant, en masse.

ii

The sky is not a dome and does not smile
its happy rays down on my naked head.
I think above this roof there is a void,
a hungry one that feeds on stars and dust.
I'll make a wager with this nothingness,
and beg the deity to come and shake
the folded rock and clay beneath my feet.

I smile to think of endless queues of souls
who wait to be rewarded or condemned
by some dyspeptic bearded man who speaks
to prophets from the whirlwind and destroys,
in fits of pique, the Cities on the Plain.
I press my palms together and breathe in
the hungry nothingness that eats my days.

iii

I pray, but never know to whom I speak—
First Cause? The silent mover who's unmoved?
A search for answers, I've been reassured,
can count for nothing in this hallowed place.
The votive candle that I've lit has burned
into a pool of wax that's dribbled down
to pit-pats on the floor. The smell remains,
mixed with a hint of polish, dust, and sweat.

How many of your followers have knelt
beneath these wooden arches, glass, and brick?
Now, conjure up their voices if you're there,
in choruses, to break my arrogance—
a childish trick, I know, of wanting proof:
a substitute for passion, pain, and grace.

Before the Papal Visit, 2015

I see, tucked in one corner of the park,
the camp of men. They sit or lean against
the chain-link fence, smoke cigarettes they've cadged
from passersby, and shout obscenities
at others of their kind who dare approach
the borders each has marked with cardboard flats,
discarded shopping carts, and clothes in heaps.

One wears a down-filled coat despite the heat.
He flashes up a sign to passing cars:
Hungry, Homeless, Veteran. They speed
their engines past this lost tribe banished to
the margins of an earth once thick with trees
where long ago with flints and snares they trapped
the horned and running game still fat with life.

At the Eastern Pennsylvania Psychiatric Institute

i

The windows here are painted shut and barred,
all mobile phones and pens locked away,
and men who never smile patrol the halls.
A poster asks, *How do you feel today?*
and illustrates this question with arrays
of faces that show sadness, guilt, and rage.
Not one of these quite comes up to my own
stew of emotions, and I'll tip my hat
to anyone who thinks they've found a match.

Do suicides show affect one can spot
(before the act of course)? Is there a face
I've passed by in a crowd that demonstrates
this principle? Can only God predict
the bearer is prepared to take the leap?

ii

My session will begin behind a door,
with noise machines to cover up my rants.
How odd we make machines that mask the sounds
of passion, while some others stoke our lusts.

Is this a rant or rave I'm hearing now?
They often are conflated, but I think
a rant shows disappointment with the world,
while any art that lives is born in raves.

My monologues so often pivot on
some memory obscure to me as well
as any therapist who listens to
my outpourings of comedy and grief,
like slinging out a catch onto a dock,
flipping, brightly scaled, and slippery.

iii

The couch inside the office lets out air
as I sink into the cushions' sticky cloth.
It seems to me that time here has been stopped
at nineteen sixty-three. The furniture
is worn, but once was *au courant*. And who
believed that my delusion could be made
much lighter with a little bit of style?
What confidence they had before the fall
in architecture, talk, and chemistry.

What keeps the staff returning here to work
each shift with addicts, narcissists, and frauds—
momentum? habit?—surely not the pay.
Reflected in the faces of them all
are signs that confidence has had its day.

iv

An Ivy-League diploma has been framed
and hung above some photographs of dogs.
The frame is cheap, the education, not.
A woman comes into the room and drops
a stack of files. She offers up her hand.

And so another therapy begins
with all the standard questions, like my age,
the status of my marriage. *I'm free.*
She asks me what's so funny. I reply,
It's nothing. Now, all irony is lost.

Of course, some things I never will reveal,
like how a dead man climbs into my bed
each night. He's not a ghost; his touch is cold.
Each night the fine silt sifts into my mouth.

Motel, Date Unknown

The air smells of ammonia. The maids
spray soap on the toilet tanks and table tops.
They push carts from room to room and sing
the madrigals that make the hours pass.

Inside a suite a man sleeps on a pile
of pillows packed around his naked thighs.
He dreams of horses grazing in a field,
who crop up grass that's vivid green and spreads

beneath the clods, the hooves, the yellow teeth.
Chains attached to bridles ring while lips
flexible as children's hands snap up
the supple strands of ripened hay and seed.

Dream on, old man; the world will inch around
the axis of its spine fifteen degrees
each hour while your phantom horses graze
around the bottles scattered on the floor.

Ignore that heart that pumps with pause and shunt,
the fractions of your days. Outside, the sun
will pass beyond the pine trees weeping pitch
on lawn chairs left to rust as seasons run.

Twelve Steps

The pipes that carry steam bang in the cold,
as if a crew of fitters hammered them.
The ceiling's high. The I-beams are exposed.
The art of the past century's revealed
to twenty souls who sit on folding chairs
and feed with coffee, cigarettes, and gum
the bodies that surround the fragile fire.

The nerves that lie beneath the outer shells
of skin and packed-in flesh are prickling
in reverent expectation of the words
that all the bodies gathered here believe
will set them free from daylight madness, sin,
the venial and the mortal kind, the past.

How odd that air compressed into a sound—
that pressure from the lungs—can have such power.
It travels from the root up to the tongue
and past the teeth. In here it's known as truth
and slippery, unlike plain honesty,
the naked lady with the crooked back.

They've gathered here, the opposites, the vain,
the queens, the rooks, the round-eyed, and the poor.
For one hour, by the stroke, the shadows stand
as if some prophet's prayer had stopped the sun.

Forest for the Trees

An invitation stands for me to pass
the forest's boundary, to make a choice
to play on lawns or venture in. A voice
pleads, *Come inside; it's cool beyond the grass.*

All night the tree roots undermine my floors.
The plaster on the ceiling heaves and falls
as shadows from the branches on the walls
send signals through the dust like semaphores.

It's not that I'm a stranger to these trees—
I've followed paths between them till I've lost
all sense of place or time. I've cut my knees

and wrists on stones and brambles till I've crossed
a trail that guided me by slow degrees
to simple daylight: hard and bright as frost.

To the Horse on Queen Lane

You shy when I approach. You know that I
will spend at least an hour here with you,
alone as always—you beyond the wire
and me with fingers slipping through the gaps.

And as I touch your neck an image comes
back from childhood; hands engraved with dirt
break up a cigarette and drop the threads
across my palm. A mouth dips down and picks
tobacco, strand by strand, with yellow teeth.

Each nostril's like a tunnel in a dream,
and underneath the massive chin are hairs
that bristle at my touch. A man whose face
is lost to memory now lifts me up
above the fence to touch the coarse dry mane,
the muscled neck—and then the image fades.

But here I am, united with my first
clear memory, on Queen Lane, standing on
the frost-heaved earth, with you, my nameless mare.
You thrust your muzzle deep into my hand
and snap up cigarettes I've broken there.

For John

I've never been inside this tiled room,
and so I must imagine drains and blood
on surfaces reflecting tubes of light
pulsing at some square-edged frame of time.

I'd say you're here, but that's not really true;
the figure laid out on the stainless steel
and zippered up in Tyvek is inert.
The vessel—as the pious texts insist—
is empty now.
                Just yesterday we spoke.
You laughed and said by Tuesday you'd be home.
Your heart was beating, pumping blood into
the storehouse in your skull: three pounds of fat
enfolding jungles, dust from stars, and words.

You once told me that immortality
exists in living memory alone;
and here you are inside my picture house.
I see you mowing grass around a hedge
while maple leaves throw shadows on your face.
You're happy now—or may I say content?

The window glass through which I watch you work
is rippled by the weight of age. It breaks
your body into facets, lines and points,
like the motions in a silent film.
The smoke that rises from your pipe jigs up
like foam that blows off from a breaking wave.

"The hours are hung with clouds, not flags"

Marilyn Hacker, "Lauds"

The light reflected from the clapboard walls
is too bright to be looked at, even now.
The grass, grown up since April, has been cut
and lies in brown and fragrant mats. The brass
is like a liquid sheet that cuts the air
as adolescent lips play fat trombones.

The trumpets and the tubas turn, left-right,
and turn again. Behind them in the fields
swallows fly in figure eights and dodge
the spinning blades of harvesters and hunt
for crickets flushed from rolling chaff and dust.

Between the orchard and the graves the brass,
the epaulettes, and braid have gathered now
to observe a voluntary. Sour notes
are choked off by the wind—or so it's been
arranged by chords of memory I own.
They're hot, these people whom I love. The crowd
fans trails of sweat from freckled arms and brows.

We pause to pray beside the stones and flags
stuck in the graves to make them sovereign states.
The dead seem more unmoved than ever. Girls
in tights and busbies toss up gilt batons,
which catch the light they hold for forty years
as shadows from the swallows pass, left-right,
across the band, the faces, and the graves.

For Christine

The paint is blistered on the chairs I've dragged
into the shade of cypresses whose scent
has reached a midday peak. Their branches sag
and brush against the grass. The heat has sent

the family's dog into the kitchen's shade.
And I've been chased off here while you rehearse.
Your notes climb up a minor scale, then fade.
I pick out snatches of a song, a verse

you've lifted from *Le Nozze*, high above
the chatter from a radio indoors:
car dealerships and weather mixed with love
and tragedy for charlatans and boors.

My thighs are fused by tree sap to the chair
as I watch mowers working through the fields.
Your muscles push out notes into the air—
a minor miracle. Your body yields

shaped air that's been compressed into a song.
Encoded in the rise and fall of sound,
the structuring of rhythm, short and long,
is some quality, elusive but profound—

an ordering of sentiment, a gift
that's given to the afternoon for free.
You start another aria and shift
a vocal run into a major key

as I watch mowers turn and cut a course
of winding stubble through the August wheat.
Your vocalizing's over, but of course
I won't forget these notes, this summer's heat.

Past Imperfect

Never again will I cross bridges
named for queens as snow begins to settle
on spreading slicks
stretched out on the Danube's flow.

I didn't know it was the last time—
why would I?—
or that I would never return,
and never again sit in a café's steam
while raincoats, shiny as tinseled trees,
passed by windows fogged by breath,
as strolling smokers paused to share a light.

Never again will I sip liquor
distilled from artichokes and feel
warmth flow back into my fingers
as I watched fox-faced girls grip
hands, pink and flushed, across a table.
One in tears, the other speaking
old words brought over the Caucasus,
which, to my untutored ear, mimicked
the cadence of peasants fiddling.

Never again will I walk gravel roads
of the humpbacked hills of Panama
with matts of decayed flowers heavy
in my lungs. Frogs croaked together
as if cued by a blind concert master
in such absolute blackness the stars
looked like a backdrop pricked
by a crew of immortal stagehands.

I stood beneath the dome and realized
its beautiful indifference as it inched
cog by cog on its nightly arc. I laughed
or cried; I can't remember which.

A Skinful

I see them on the trains. Their skin and hair
is smooth below the pulsing light. Their clothes
reveal the fineness of their bones. They stare
at nothing, deep in private music, posed
in attitudes that speak indifference to
the din, the clicking trainmen, or their mates,
whose elbows touch. I know there's something new
in this closing of experience. I rate
a glance and nothing more. Thus, I'm allowed
an observation of the faces here.
Unlike my own, they're free of lines. Their brows
are smooth and white—untroubled by the fear
I travel with as my companion. They
rock gently on their bones as bodies sway.

ii

My skin renews itself. Old layers slough
away in showers, soap and steam. My face
remains the same face, nonetheless—enough
alike at least for me to see the place
where it was cut when I was ten. It's strange
how faces can remember what they are;
how all the little cells are so arranged
that they emerge unblemished or as scars.
What is this memory? Where is it stored?
is there some ideal template of my skin,

a mask that I'm condemned to wear? If bored
at looking at the features I live in,
I know that age will pull them to the bone
in lines and crows' feet—lichens rimed on stone.

iii

How odd to realize all thoughts within
the frame of opaque bones and fragile cells
wrapped up inside the stretched and prickled skin
will only live as long we ourselves.
This remnant of a sea inside a sack,
this ghost of pressure balanced by the air
and tension from the water pushing back
that each of us has been condemned to wear,
will break down into nothing, given time.
The shell that holds all grief and memory,
in chains of molecules that make a mind,
will turn back into atoms, hungry, free.
We're spirits caught inside our skin and hair—
ephemeral our dramas, spun from air.

Photograph, W. H. Auden, 1972

The light is from three-quarters back and hard.
It's not flattering to a face that's lined
and made heavy from years of drink and smoke.
His skin's, in fact, remarkably like stone
that's weathered on an outcrop or a ledge.
And that's a fact remarkable because
he once had written poetry in praise
of limestone that had softened into forms
resembling human arms, and legs, and sex,
on which some naked boys had come to play
and make a show of bodies young and fresh.

But limestone makes, I think he noted then,
a landscape that is feminine in form—
Like mother, were his words. I'm now convinced
this poem's real beauty comes from need
instead of observation. And his face
is more like weathered stone than any boy's.

A face that's not a mask but is a place
that ruin is projected on. And pain
has burrowed hard beneath the softened points
of flesh and muscle and the web of nerves
that move and breathe beneath the hardened skin.

I have another picture of him young.
The face is smooth and looks as if he's tried
to hide inside that smoothness, barbered hair,
and old-boy tie he wore habitually.
And I suspect he's wearing skin that's loose
and not just in a photograph but in
the paradise of old men, and I pray
the landscape that he loved is heaven's too.

Photograph, Anne Sexton, 1973

She's caught inside a sudden burst of light,
an incandescent pop, a brilliant cone
that pours into the shadows of the room
and washes all the texture from her face.
This magnitude of light can be a shock,
can burn into the retina of the eye
and leave behind a violet smear that hangs
inside the bitter humor of the ball.

She looks up from her paper straight at us—
all those who want a picture with their words.
And this is what she looks like: middle aged;
her hands look even older, but she's still
attractive in her confidence. She's spread
some manuscripts and pens across the desk,
and waves a cigarette just like a star.

In this small room the craft of poetry
is tempered by a woman's troubled roles
as artist, daughter, wife. Does she look mad,
this former mental patient who now writes?
Historically, she would be thought possessed
and put through trials to prove her innocence.
How things have changed; no one would do that now.
They gave her all the therapy she'd take,
both individually or in a group,
and miracles encoded into pills.

Photograph, T. S. Eliot, 1932

The figures on the lawn are shadowless.
The women wear straw hats to keep the heat
from prickling their skin. The poet's dressed
in tweed; the pieces are well-cut and hold
his figure firm from shoes to knotted tie.

The women on his flank don't even try
to show some pleasure at this chance to be
immortalized. In fact, they look annoyed
to be out posing on a lawn that's rolled
and clipped so close and carefully it looks
as if some clever hands had woven it.

More ironical than amused, the poet's smile
suggests that we're intruded on his time.
His hosts stand right behind playing bowls.
And yet I can't imagine he might join
their game with jacket off and loosened tie,
with rings of sweat that spreads beneath his arms,
or yelling out in triumph when he knocks
another player's ball out of the pitch.
I doubt his joy could ever be expressed
with hot-stoked blood, with pumping arms and fists.

In a Room of Quaker Plainness

They gather on the frozen ground and push
their fingers through the gaps between the wire.
The shadows from the mesh fall on each face
that looks out through the scratches and the clumps
of grit, the washed-out celluloid that stares
directly from the screen into my eyes.
The clattering of sprockets fills the room.
Projected light divides and strikes the dust
that drifts in eddies through the air like smoke.

A girl who sits one row behind me weeps.
I raise my hand; projected on my skin
are images from death camps, shrunken down.
The picture jumps and stutters on a splice,
then cuts. And now on screen a man pops lice
from the collar of his shirt with cigarettes.
He wears his skin so loosely that the wind
blows right through it and shifts his bones as well.
He looks up at the camera's lens and grins.

Old men and women dressed in winter coats
are forced at rifle point to watch as gangs
of kapos stack the heaps of dead by sex.
White ash or snowflakes settle on their hats,
their uniforms, their shoulder boards, their boots.
A tractor shoves the tumbling dead to pits,
as shadow people gather around a truck,
and soldiers hand out bowls of steaming mush.

A sergeant—by his stripes—looks out at me.
He's angry and embarrassed, wants to know
the answers to the questions no one asks.
The shadow on his face, like mine, is set.

Photograph, Liberia, 1980

Along a beach posts have been driven,
one every forty feet, as if for telephones,
and indeed, wires have been strung,
but instead of crossbars and insulators
they wrap the torsos of half-naked men,
cutting arms and bundling chests,
making them look like capons trussed for braising.

A soldier in fatigues and cap scratches
his head with a pistol while guarding
the men on the posts, his prisoners,
who've been rousted from their beds at dawn
to come to this beach with its flies, tires,
and fish frames wrapped in kelp
and become part of history.

The men on the posts are oddly passive—
to my viewer's eyes, resigned, like people
waiting to draw cash or board a bus.
But I, and the men on the beach, know
they are going to die.
*Government Officials deposed in a coup
and executed for the cameras
of the foreign press,* the caption reads.

The soldier's fingers wrap
the butt of his shiny pistol.
He, or one like him, will do it.
Drawing back the oily slide
of his weighty little machine,
feeling the action thrust a bullet,
tight and fresh, into the chamber.

Sand chuffs under his boots. Twill,
damp with sweat and spray,
makes a light whisking sound
as he strolls to the far end of the line.
The heads of his prisoners follow him
as if by reflex, then look down.

Camera shutters chatter.
Flashes pock sand and skin.
The pop of the pistol is muted,
but the pull of the bodies' weight
runs down the wire. One man,
the late minister of health,
twitches involuntarily,
and for that gets a volley.

Birds fly flat over the water.
Photographers and pressmen retire
to file early. A stale smell drifts
down the beach, not of death (not yet),
but of urine, brackish, fear.

Prayers mix with the sound of the lapping tide.
Inland, a truck climbing a hill down-shifts.
A woman and child count to a hundred in English.
A plea drops from a cabinet minister's lips
and luffs off in a gust of wind.

The pistol snaps open, empty, smoking.
The minister says, *Oh, my brother?*
As the soldier thumbs a fresh cartridge
against a spring, he fumbles it and it rolls
against the feet of the bound man.

The soldier has to touch those feet
to retrieve the bullet,
begins to ask the minister's pardon,
but seeing piss spread across his britches
chokes off his apology.
A man should not do this,
he whispers to himself,
to the dead and to the living.

Fall Back

A bullet spins from rifled steel
at sixteen hundred feet per second,
faster than thought,
and, like speech,
there's no taking it back.
What's the impulse to squeeze
a finger against burled metal—
which is, after all, just a lever?

*Give me where to stand
and I will move the earth.*

Fall back before the impulse and the twitch—
back to when the barrel and the stock
were drawn from a leather case,
back to when the cardboard box
was taken from a shelf:
Hollow points? Jacketed?
The glow of brass, the oily smell
familiar from those mornings
of rising before first light
and pulling on canvas pants
stiff from last year's rain and muck.

Back to dreams of wading out to sea
with brine breaking around your shins.
Shadows pass beneath palm trees
beneath an unforgiving sun.
You see clouds bunched up and pass
across a purple land as thin
as a thumbnail on a false horizon. . . .
Back to the playground's blacktop where
the summer's heat is so intense
that you can push a snail's shell deep
into the bubbling tar.

Back to the maddening *thump-thump*
of basketballs as you play alone.
And somewhere over the horizon
you hear a rifle's crack.

Bankrupt Farms

I was given the old boots for nothing—
black and slick as a seal's muzzle.
All March the cracked rubber leaked in slush
as I tramped the bushed-out flats
and bogs, navigating with the balls
of my feet and chance, following the ruts

between strands of rusted wire, ruts
filled with tires and oil seepage. Nothing
remained of the farm's stock but bones. A ball
joint exposed, dug out by the muzzles
of the skeletal dogs who patrolled the flat
field's borders, whose tracks I saw in slush

running in pairs. Their yellow marks in slush,
often still steaming in the ruts.
Once, I found one shot, and lying flat—
a new mother, nipples extended, nothing
remained of her head but the muzzle's
grinning jaw, and socket where the ball

of her eye once opened. No ball-
fetcher this one, whose grave in slush
no child mourned, or stroked her muzzle
in remembrance. Her pups left in a rut
for crows, marauding males, and the nothing
of hunger, the long echo, the flat

silence. And at the road's end, a flat-
roofed farmhouse, buckled like a puffball
squashed by a giant's daughter. Nothing
remained but fly-specked curtains, slush,
a jar of fossils, gathered from ruts.
Pansies with withered muzzles

were left by a wedding dress on a rifle's muzzle,
like a mannequin stained and flattened
by rain. I'd often jumped from rut to rut
when the fields were washed to lakes of slush,
gathered like a weight of loss, a ball
of failure on a flat trajectory; nothing

but stillbirth, that hardness in the muzzle, a charity ball
packed up and gone; flat furrows in slush.
Nothing but bones washed in spring rains from ruts.

Prologue for an Imaginary Play

Imagine, now, a forest of young trees.
They've grown so close together
that their branches interleave. Their bark is smooth
except in places where long fissures
have erupted on their skins. They ease out sap
which dribbles on the branches and the roots.
Pay close attention to them, they're the stage
on which our little drama will be played.

Imagine that you're in this forest now,
and whichever way you walk, the needle on
your compass swings around and points back to
the place from which you came, as if these trees
were standing at the true magnetic north.
You stop to catch your breath and realize
that all the trees around you are the same
in height and width and age as well as type.

Imagine that you're young again, so young
that you can feel the beating of your heart:
the pause, the shunt, the pressure from the pump
that pushes through your fingers, eyes, and lungs.
And with each step your feet stir up the scent
of living things: the spores from trampled ferns,
and mats of rotted nuts and broken leaves
which mask the sour scent of human fear.

Imagine that each minute that you're here
inside this forest, all your memories
of sunlight, home, and family start to slip—
you can't remember any place outside
a path beneath this canopy of trees.
Your breath is mixed up with the living air—
the dripping sap, the spores, and rotted leaves.
You close your eyes and all you see are trees.

August 1963

The clouds look brighter mirrored in the lake
than when I look at them with just my eyes,
as if the water were a photograph
whose edges frame the sky against the black
and stagnant water, weeds, and earthen dam.
Sunfish lie in rows along the dock.
Their gills blow up to violet as they draw
the lethal oxygen into their lungs.

My mother and her husband have gone off
into the trees that line the other shore;
they left an hour ago. I shield my eyes
to see if I can find the path they took,
but trunks and branches form a wall of gray.

I sink a hook into a minnow's back—
I'm not allowed to use the hand-tied lures,
the spinners or the flies. The dying fish
is fighting in my hand. Its blood runs pink,
and smells as if an ocean were inside.
I press my thumb against the barb and draw
the point into the callus on my skin.
A single drop of blood wells on the steel.

I can't forget my mother's in the woods
with him beneath the cool indifferent trees.
I shield my eyes and scan the other shore,
but there's no sign of movement in the woods.
The contrail of a passing jet reflects
a spreading ribbon stretched across the lake.
I cast into the center of the pool
And watch the vapor spread apart in waves.

My mother and her husband reappear
behind a clump of alders by the dam.
He holds a bramble back for her to pass.
Her sneaker slips into the lake. She cries.
He grabs her hand and helps her up the bank.

There's something secretive about them both.
They laugh. Their legs are bare. Their arms are tan.
What color would they turn under the trees?
A rhododendron's dark and slippery green,
or like the mast of leaves spread on the ground?
My mother waves and calls out, *Any luck?*
I don't reply. I watch them cross the dam
and help each other balance on the rocks
while carrying secrets on their backs like weights.

September 11, 1973

for Vic

Where did you go that day? You were in bed,
the corporeal you I mean, raddled down
to an envelope around a frame of bones—
but recognizable. That other you,
the lover of political discourse,
off beats, and sly guitars had gone away.
A rationalist would claim that you'd dissolved
into a soup of chemistry and lost
the spark between the fragile points that glow
and make a living being. But, of course,
how much of life is really rational?

Your aunts in Carolina and Ponce
don't buy this argument; they say your ghost
looked back as it ascended high above
the mourners with no mourning left to give:
the ones who'd watched you lie for months inside
a private world of pain while trembling,
your eyes pressed down by morphine's gentle weight.

So what do I believe while I tack down
these words—that you are somewhere in the clouds?
I wish I could, but there's a stubborn part
that won't believe your spirit's found a home
in heaven—but I'll set aside my doubts
for just this hour in memory of you.

What sort of conversations do you have
in your dimension? Do you speak in prose?
There must be animals up there with you.
When young, I couldn't make myself believe
they had no souls. It seemed to me their souls
were held so close beneath the rim
that I could see them stirring in the sphere.

Do they lie down on sunlit grass that's lush—
raccoons or feral cats, and snuffling hounds,
and buffalos with shaggy mats of fur
who shake off flies that circle round their heads?
I see you there among them on a hill,
beneath some flowering chestnuts, reading Marx.

Song

I step out on the street and disappear.
Inside my room I feel the boards secured
beneath my feet in mortises and joints.
But in the air the sunlight passes straight
between the stitch and counter-stitch and heats
my long articulated bones.

I pass others with their faces set
against the shock and counter-shock, and trained,
by habit I suppose, to seal themselves
against the press of phones and painted shoes,
the flannel, and the swinging leather bags,
and only feet are seen below the mass.

A girl jogs up. Her wet, pink skin is stretched
around her moving frame. She's bound up tight—
compressed inside her flesh and stripped to fight.
She looks as if she'd like to break through me
and all the other people in her path
but is constrained by numbers, if not time.

She's angry, but pure body in her rage:
big fleshed, as if her spirit's shrunken down
as both her arms and thighs have been pumped and flexed.
She stamps down from the paving to the street
while muttering a private curse at birds
who've gathered at some broken bread to feed.

The Poles believe that city birds are souls
of those who died before they found true love.
The count, great as it is, is far too low;
they'd make a lonely city to themselves—
an aerial Manhattan or Lublin—
and fight for castoffs dropped onto the streets.

I step out of my door and disappear.
Inside my room I feel the boards secured
beneath my feet in mortises and joints.
But in the air the sunlight passes straight
between the stitch and counter-stitch and heats
my long articulated bones.

Old Bones

The origin of music, it's believed,
began in innocence when someone drilled
stops that turned a bone into a flute—
forgetting, if you will, the desperate wheeze
of old men breathing out their last, the thwack
of cobbles flaking blades from cores of flint,
the hiss of pine knots laid on coals, the keen
of birthing women breaching their laments.

But bones don't last where flies and grubs bore through
the filigrees of calcium, while leaves
leech acid through on matrices of hips,
teeth, and femurs. Exhumed, white shrouds reveal
faint shadows left by faces of the dead,
but of the hollow bones there's not a trace.

An Early Recording

The couple sitting next to me who've strung
their headsets into laptops aren't aware
that, in the dark above them, speakers play
recordings of John Coltrane's fat-belled horn.
He burns though "Good Bait," while Red Garland vamps
his modes around the sticks of Philly Joe,
and high-hats past Ron Carter. "Take me home."
Like other customers I've sealed myself
against the rawness of experience
behind these observations, boxed in words.

And so I close my eyes and through the smoke
watch derby lights spin gels of blue and green.
Polished brass and ebony reflect
the faces of the customers who watch
a man blow though his tenor southern light
that's pitiless in August—cottonwoods
stand in sharp relief against the rows
of houses jacked on pilings, stoked with blood.

Between the Hours

i

My wife lies in a heavy musk, cocooned
by quilted blankets, sheets, and bed. The room
is never really dark; the streetlights bleed
vapor light on furniture and floors,
reducing her into a mass of spheres:
hips, shoulders, head, and breasts—the curves that hold
in muscles, bones, and heart, the dreaming brain
dropped nightly down into a little death.

This is the hour I feel contempt for all
my systems of philosophy and words
which have reverted back to sounds: to *ah's*
and *oo's*—the *t's* that tap against the teeth
and thicken tongues. But for this hour I'll speak
the fluent tongues passed down from paradise.

ii

Ghosts thrived in gaslight; gaps of air inside
the lines that fed the lamps made shadows shift,
revealing, in a corner of an eye,
a moving hand, a loosened strand of hair
above a sad or grinning face—and please
let's not forget the patient hunger there.
When power lines were strung from house to house
and light, at last, became reliable,
spirits became obscure to us, except

inside the attics in our heads.
                                        One night
my sister showed up in a dream. She wept,
or laughed—I can't know which precisely—
nails bitten to the quick, still bearing scars,
some visible to me and others not.

iii

Now in all innocence the sleepers drift
above the roofs, or lead the orchestras
while naked on the podiums. These dreams
flow tumbling down from beds in clinging musk
which pools on rugs or inches up the floor,
then trickles under cracks again at dawn.
Night, who always walks in woman's form,
or so I'm told, now draws a fearful pact
to make me face these stolid hours alone.

In rows of houses, sleepers lie at peace
beside their dreaming wives, oblivious
as men with microphones confront the waves
that lash at waterfronts inside a world
made up of prickled skin and aching bone.

Strange Obsequies

Even in August the chapel's cold.
Stones sweat, and only the bench rails,
polished to a blond grain, feel warm.
Hymnals, with today's program, are stored
on the backs of pews—bright red.

I've been here before, but never in this state,
reduced (at God knows what temperature)
to lumps of ash. So how, how do I see?
Spirits, in conventions handed down
by all the master liars and the Gospels, see.
But with what eyes, rolled in sockets
by watch-maker muscles, do I see?
I should be hovering at the back, high
above these heads, bare or thickly covered—
the young with hair like fur, the old
with oily bands dragged across their scalps—
but find myself among these mourners—small,
like a child of ten. We kneel for prayer.
The rail, though padded, still feels hard,
reminding me of knees I no longer have.
Standing now, I scan the crowd for tears,
but grief, as always, is swallowed here.

We move off in files: cousins—*cousins?*—
and spirits, some transparent, others
solid as bones in tailored clothes;
dead women! *How nice of you to come,*
I thought; *well never mind*—
through an allée of yews (the one cliché

I allow). The sky is hazy-bright;
no rain, battalions of massed umbrellas,
idling limousines, hysteria, or tulle,
just shadows on the sandy ground,
an urn, like a can for tea, and oh,
my family agreeing to be unlike themselves
for two hours, exactly.

Elegy for Maureen Holm

The Chinese sages once imagined earth
not only flat, but square,
with mountains at each corner to hold
the heavens up, like tent poles.
Once the earth had been heaven's reflection,
but had grown uncertain and distraught.
Souls made their way to paradise, like Dante,
by climbing mountains and passing through fire.

Can I imagine Heaven not square
but perfectly disordered?
A sandstone Manhattan where oranges
are given to each passenger on the subway.
Where investment bankers apologize
to perfect strangers for what they do.
Where saints live tethered in balloons
and bless fleets of taxicabs
whose drivers wear wigs that smell of coconut
and outdo each other in small courtesies.
Where a soldier's only duty
is to come home and be kissed.
Where the tunnels are made of glass
and open onto fields of sedum.

A Heaven where you are crowned
with strawberry leaves. And all-night banquets
are spread on parkland in your honor.
Where the speakers are Rilke and Rimbaud,
who dare a sleeping populace
to make you Supreme Grammarian,
and the Mayor promptly obliges.

Meetings with My Father

i

He's tall, this man I've never seen before.
His body tapers up to thinning hair.
He holds a present in his hand, a poor
dead caiman that's been stuffed with straw. I stare

into the grinning teeth, then back away.
The man talks to my mother but ignores
the children gathered in the room. We play
the game of passing signals that the bores

who talk above our heads don't ever see.
I notice that the lizard's patterned skin
is stenciled with gold letters. There are three
of us and one toy. We begin

to win the stranger's favor with our eyes.
Ignored—but we've been taught to be polite.
Hello from Sunny Florida! the prize.
I'm youngest here and know there'll be a fight

to claim it when my mother is away.
But even so, I don't give up the game
of winning something I don't want. We play
the roles that always are the same,

and will be all our lives, but we don't know
this yet, and maybe never will: *Scapegoat,
Hero, Mascot*—how odd this doesn't show
to adults. Now the stranger gets his coat

and leaves. He takes the toy along with him,
without once ever looking at my face.
And yet somehow his visit doesn't dim;
some fold inside my head tricks time and space.

ii

The kitchen is pitched hot against the cold.
The windows steam. My father's second wife
is wrapped up in a quilted robe—it's old
and frayed around the hem. She takes a knife

and slices bacon. Fat smokes in a pan.
She's half awake, yet trying to be kind.
But breakfast isn't in my father's plan.
We're headed out again. I can't unwind

the cord that's knotted in my gut. The dog
is shivering and radiates the stink
of something foul she's rolled in, like a bog.
I stretch, and pour cold coffee out. The sink

is filled with grouse and pheasant cocks. Their blood
is gathering in pools around the drain,
and spattered on my jacket, mixed with mud.
Outside, the porch roof rattles, drummed by rain.

The pleasant smell of gun oil's on my skin:
a scent that always takes me to this hour
of heat inside the kitchen. We begin
to hitch up boots and canvas pants. The sour

reek of gutted pheasants fills the air,
and makes me happy that it's finally time
to head back to the fields. But I don't dare
to lead. I rise and follow. Now we climb

a hill through stubbled corn. The rain's begun
in earnest. We're spread out across the fields.
My fingers burn. I've yet to fire my gun.
We're out till dark. My father never yields.

iii

It's Friday night. You've brought my sister back
from college for the weekend, but she's shut
herself behind a bedroom door. You track
your boots across the hardwood floor and strut

around the rooms as if you owned them. Ask
my mother what she pays in rent. Your voice
is overloud. You've slipped behind the mask
I know from long experience: a choice

(to my regret I later will repeat)
of feigning unconcern for pain and fear—
a family disease; it's taken neat
or fortified, like now, with shots and beer.

As always, you are putting effort in
the pose of being intelligent and tough.
I once admired this. Now you begin
to tease us for our poverty. *Enough!*

I never say it, but I wished you'd go,
and drag the scent of man along with you.
The rain that came with you has turned to snow
that streaks along the windows. Now the blue

and hazy streetlight flickers off and on.
You'll have to drive an hour in the dark.
Decline another coffee. Then you're gone.
Your boots track back to where your car is parked.

You wipe the windshield with your fist and drive.
My sister comes out from her room. It's plain
she's frightened—says she's glad to be alive.
I watch your tracks dissolve. Snow turns to rain.

iv

To get to you I've hitched across the state—
one day and night, but back here in the woods
surrounded by your dogs, I hesitate
to intrude on your privacy. I should

have bunked down with some friends not far from here.
But I have been provided with a bed
dragged out onto the porch. The night is clear.
Your dogs run back and forth on chains. Instead

of sleeping I'm lying here awake
and staring at the wheelchair where your wife
now spends her days. Last night I watched you take
an hour to feed her, spoon by spoon—a life

now circumscribed between your farmhouse walls.
The clothes and soiled sheets that show your care
are cracking in the wind on lines. It falls
on you to wash and hang them in the air.

It only took me six rides to arrive,
with dead hours in between each. So I guess
some God I never thank keeps me alive
for reasons still obscure to me. I bless

the smell of grass, the dogs on chains who run
the hours out, but what about the man
whose blood is partly mine, who calls me son?
(A title that surprises me.) I can

with all my self-control suppress a smile
when so addressed. I'll hitch out after ten—
the old man's been impatient for a while.
How strange to think we'll never meet again.

v

I've come home late from dinner when my wife
calls down, *You'd better listen to this now.*
Another birthday's knocked away. My life
has tipped the half-way point. I don't know how

four decades have gone by me in a blur.
I don't sleep well at night, but find relief
in frost distilled. I pour some out and stir
in ice; tipped back, it falls against my teeth.

Upstairs I see the light on the machine
flash off and on. I shuttle back, and hear
my father's voice break through the hiss. I lean
in close, adjust the volume till it's clear.

I wish that we were closer. He sounds weak,
unlike the person that I used to know—
constrained, as if a stone had tried to speak.
He's never said these words before. Although

we haven't seen each other face to face
in years, I must admit I feel remorse
that we are strangers now. It's not a case
of cool indifference on my part. Of course

our histories makes it difficult to say
six words that aren't trivial aloud.
I shuttle back the message, then hit *Play*
and listen to his voice again. This proud

old veteran's been reduced by loneliness
or guilt to try to reach me through the wire.
I finish off my drink, start to undress,
erase the message—putting out a fire.

Last Wish

I wish that all the hours I've spent with bores
in heated arguments were mine again.
I'd pack them in a cooler for the shore—
the precious minutes chilled like frosted gin.

Beyond the dunes I'd spread a blanket out
and watch the bobbing heads as old men swim.
Quick shadows fall from kites as children shout
and run along the breaking foam and skim.

And feeling generous I'd freely give
some fifteen minutes that I've stashed away
to anyone I fancied—let them live
or squander what they have before the day

has swallowed them in traffic, noise and heat,
or passed them by in heartache, beat by beat.

After working for three decades in film production, Rob Wright has now chosen to spend his time writing. He currently serves as associate fiction editor for *Able Muse*, and has been awarded three Fellowships in Literature from the Pennsylvania Council on the Arts. He has twice been nominated for the Pushcart Prize, and has published fiction, reviews, and poetry in *Able Muse, Angle, Big City Lit*, the *Evansville Review, Measure, Rattle, String Poet*, and the *Schuylkill Valley Journal*. A finalist for the Howard Nemerov Sonnet Award, he recently was awarded the Frost Farm Prize for Metrical Poetry and was honored to give a reading at the home of Frost in Derry, New Hampshire.

ALSO FROM ABLE MUSE PRESS

Jacob M. Appel, *The Cynic in Extremis – Poems*

William Baer, *Times Square and Other Stories;*
 New Jersey Noir – A Novel;
 New Jersey Noir (Cape May) – A Novel;

Lee Harlin Bahan, *A Year of Mourning (Petrarch) – Translation*

Melissa Balmain, *Walking in on People (Able Muse Book Award for Poetry)*

Ben Berman, *Strange Borderlands – Poems;*
 Figuring in the Figure – Poems

David Berman, *Progressions of the Mind – Poems*

Lorna Knowles Blake, *Green Hill (Able Muse Book Award for Poetry)*

Michael Cantor, *Life in the Second Circle – Poems*

Catherine Chandler, *Lines of Flight – Poems*

William Conelly, *Uncontested Grounds – Poems*

Maryann Corbett, *Credo for the Checkout Line in Winter – Poems;*
 Street View – Poems
 In Code – Poems

Will Cordeiro, *Trap Street (Able Muse Book Award for Poetry)*

John Philip Drury, *Sea Level Rising – Poems*

Rhina P. Espaillat, *And After All – Poems*

Anna M. Evans, *Under Dark Waters: Surviving the* Titanic *– Poems*

D. R. Goodman, *Greed: A Confession – Poems*

Carrie Green, *Studies of Familiar Birds – Poems*

Margaret Ann Griffiths, *Grasshopper – The Poetry of M A Griffiths*

Katie Hartsock, *Bed of Impatiens – Poems*

Elise Hempel, *Second Rain – Poems*

Jan D. Hodge, *Taking Shape – carmina figurata;*
 The Bard & Scheherazade Keep Company – Poems

Ellen Kaufman, *House Music – Poems*
 Double-Parked, with Tosca – Poems

Emily Leithauser, *The Borrowed World (Able Muse Book Award for Poetry)*

Hailey Leithauser, *Saint Worm – Poems*

Carol Light, *Heaven from Steam – Poems*

Kate Light, *Character Shoes – Poems*

April Lindner, *This Bed Our Bodies Shaped – Poems*

Martin McGovern, *Bad Fame – Poems*

Jeredith Merrin, *Cup – Poems*

Richard Moore, *Selected Poems;*
The Rule That Liberates: An Expanded Edition – Selected Essays

Richard Newman, *All the Wasted Beauty of the World – Poems*

Alfred Nicol, *Animal Psalms – Poems*

Deirdre O'Connor, *The Cupped Field (Able Muse Book Award for Poetry)*

Frank Osen, *Virtue, Big as Sin (Able Muse Book Award for Poetry)*

Alexander Pepple (Editor), *Able Muse Anthology;*
Able Muse – a review of poetry, prose & art (semiannual, winter 2010 on)

James Pollock, *Sailing to Babylon – Poems*

Aaron Poochigian, *The Cosmic Purr – Poems;*
Manhattanite (Able Muse Book Award for Poetry)

Tatiana Forero Puerta, *Cleaning the Ghost Room – Poems*

Jennifer Reeser, *Indigenous – Poems*

John Ridland, *Sir Gawain and the Green Knight (Anonymous) – Translation;*
Pearl (Anonymous) – Translation

Stephen Scaer, *Pumpkin Chucking – Poems*

Hollis Seamon, *Corporeality – Stories*

Ed Shacklee, *The Blind Loon: A Bestiary*

Carrie Shipers, *Cause for Concern (Able Muse Book Award for Poetry)*

Matthew Buckley Smith, *Dirge for an Imaginary World (Able Muse Book Award for Poetry)*

Susan de Sola, *Frozen Charlotte – Poems*

Barbara Ellen Sorensen, *Compositions of the Dead Playing Flutes – Poems*

Rebecca Starks, *Time Is Always Now – Poems;*
Fetch Muse – Poems

Sally Thomas, *Motherland – Poems*

J.C. Todd, *Beyond Repair – Poems*

Paulette Demers Turco (Editor), *The Powow River Poets Anthology II*

Rosemerry Wahtola Trommer, *Naked for Tea – Poems*

Wendy Videlock, *Slingshots and Love Plums – Poems;*
The Dark Gnu and Other Poems;
Nevertheless – Poems

Richard Wakefield, *A Vertical Mile – Poems;*
Terminal Park – Poems

Gail White, *Asperity Street – Poems*

Chelsea Woodard, *Vellum – Poems*

www.ablemusepress.com